FAVOURITE
AUSTRALIAN POEMS

FAVOURITE
AUSTRALIAN POEMS

Paintings by Rex Newell

Introduction by
Chris Mansell

NEW
HOLLAND

CONTENTS

A.B. PATERSON

Known as 'The Banjo of the Bush' Andrew Barton Paterson is the author of Australia's national song, 'Waltzing Matilda', and a great many other classic Australian verses.

Born in the bush (just out of Orange) in 1864, he moved to Sydney and later worked as a solicitor before his verses became well known (at first to readers of *The Bulletin* and later through his books).

When he became successful and popular as a writer, and his real identity became known, he let his legal career lapse and became, among other things, a war correspondent for *The Sydney Morning Herald* during the Boer War and a serving member of the AIF in the First World War, where he rose to the rank of Captain.

At home he was the editor of several major newspapers at one time or another. But Paterson was a vigorous man, a sporting man who loved horses, who worked in cities but loved to go back to the country and to experience country life. In many ways he was what contemporary Australian men aspire to be, writ large.

Australians will always have a fondness for Paterson, not least because he chose as his pseudonym ('Banjo') the name of a horse he once rode.

'Out Back' ('The old year went, and the new returned, in the withering weeks of drought...') can only bring a shudder of recognition to those on the land.

Lawson saw himself as truly a poet of the people. He had a sad, troubled life, with illness and alcohol overtaking him in the end, but his poems and stories have shaped the way Australians have thought about themselves now for generations.

GEORGE ESSEX EVANS

George Essex Evans is probably the only Australian poet for whom a pilgrimage is made to his monument every year. Although his well-crafted work is fondly regarded throughout Australia, it is in Queensland, especially Toowoomba where he finally lived and died, that Essex Evans is esteemed above all other bush poets.

Although born in Scotland, he became a fully-fledged 'banana bender' when he became editor of *The Queenslander* after trying farming and a stint as a teacher. During his lifetime three collections of his poems were published: *The Repentance of Magdalene Despar; Loraine, and Other Verses;* and *The Secret Kay and Other Verses,* which was published three years before his death in 1909.

The Women of the West is George Essex Evans' best known and loved poem. It is a great favourite throughout Australia. The poem is a tribute to the often forgotten and invisible women of the bush who made the homes and endured great hardship in bringing up children and working on the land beside the men.

HENRY LAWSON

Henry Lawson was born in a tent in the gold-diggings just outside Grenfell, New South Wales, in 1867 to Louisa Lawson, who was to become an outstanding journalist and feminist of her day.

Lawson was modest in character, nearly deaf since childhood and shy by nature but with a passion for justice and a knack with people. He was a man who deeply believed that all were equal. He wrote at a time when Australians were much concerned with social issues, and when the basis for contemporary Australia was established.

His visions in verse and stories have become the defining way to see some of our past, and some of our present. 'The Teams' still remains the best picture of a bullock-team, and the opening line of

C.J. DENNIS

'I dips me lid, and stands aside', wrote Henry Lawson of C.J. Dennis in 1915 in the language of Dennis' Sentimental Bloke. Indeed, none can match the bloke laureate in this sort of poetry and Dennis—known as Den—made his fortune and his reputation from the publication of 'The Sentimental Bloke'.

It was just as well. Den had started *The Gadfly*, and saw it go bust. He wrote his best known piece while he was living in an old tram parked on a friend's property. At 38 he was broke and depressed. Three years later he had a national reputation and affluence to match.

But Den wrote much more than The Bloke. He had 'kicked around', he said, quite a bit after he left his father's home in South

Australia at 21. In the flesh, he was no Ginger Mick. He was a writer through and through and had many of the failings of writers. More than once Mrs Dennis had to put his head under the cold tap to sober him up enough to get to the next deadline. But he managed to make a living in Australia as a poet and a writer—no mean achievement even now—and to invent characters that we still know and love.

BARNEY O'TOOLE

Barney O'Toole published very few poems but his 'When the Teams Brought in the Wool' has the authentic ring of the bullocky's life. This world has largely passed away, although there are still some who can drive a team, dig it out if necessary, and probably write a poem about it afterwards. It certainly still lives in the imaginations of both rural and urban Australians.

'When the Teams Brought in the Wool' embodies the familiar Australian ethic of 'She'll be right Jack'—often misinterpreted as a lazy, lackadaisical, good-for-nothing-much attitude. In reality it is an ability to get on with the hardships of life and work without fuss or undue drama—but often with a touch, or more than a touch, of humour. Or beer. Or both.

It is a can-do attitude that O'Toole expresses in the last line of the poem: 'He simply took the good with the bad, and brought the woolclip down'. Embodied so neatly in a bullocky's tale this ethic has served Australians well from Gallipoli to the present.

HENRY KENDALL

Kendall was a native born Australian who drew his inspiration and images from the land of his birth, and had a different temper from many of the other poets writing about the bush. Born in 1839 at Kirmington in the coastal district of Ulladulla in New South Wales, he went to sea in his teens for two years before returning to work in the city, Scone and then Melbourne.

'Bell-Birds' is a poem many Australians can still recite today. It doesn't speak of the hardships of the land or the dusty loneliness of the outback, but of the cool, watered coastal landscape in which Kendall himself found solace. It is softer and quieter than the rollicking ballads of many of his contemporaries.

This is a reflection of the man. Although he had many supporters and some patrons (Henry Parkes, Premier of New South Wales and architect of Federation among them) he was quieter, more solitary and more introspective than most.

Unlike much bush verse, it is the land itself, not the people, real or imaginary, that preoccupied Kendall. It was Kendall, more than others, who began to teach Australians to appreciate the beauty of their own land.

WILL OGILVIE

Born in Scotland, Ogilvie was drawn to Australia in 1889 by his love of adventure. In fact, he spent 12 years in the outback, experiencing the life first hand, mustering, horsebreaking and droving for Belalie Station on the Warrego River and in South Australia.

It was not unusual in the mid to late 1800s for Scottish lads to come to Australia to seek adventure and fortune. Many made the fortunes, and a large proportion of them stayed to contribute to what has become Australian culture as we know it. Ogilvie had been drawn here by his admiration for another icon of Australian poetry, Adam Lindsay Gordon.

Like many of the best bush poets, his work was published in *The Bulletin*. His classic droving poem 'From the Gulf' is a great example of what the Australian ballad can be. He had a strong male voice—in the tradition of bush verse—but he was also famous for his softer, romantic poems.

Unlike most, Ogilvie was to return to Scotland, although he continued to write of his Australian experiences in poems and in the story of his Australian adventures, *My Life in the Open,* which was published in 1908.

THOMAS E. SPENCER

Australia has long been proud of its cricketing abilities—its flamboyant, or at least unusual, characters and the team's ability to win through (even if, as is the case in Spencer's most famous poem, it is with a little help from our canine friends).

Originally a Londoner, Thomas Spencer came to Australia when he was 18 years of age and returned to settle in Sydney in 1875. He was a man who liked to work with his hands, and was a builder by trade, although he had published two books of poetry and a novel, as well as a number of short stories in *The Bulletin*.

'How McDougall Topped the Score' is his best loved poem. It is often recited in pubs and lounge rooms today along with 'Why Doherty Died'. The ingenious spirit, combined with an interest in anything to do with cricket, was bound to make McDougall a folk hero. Spencer's poem celebrates the bush talent for improvising clever and unexpected ways to bring down an opponent. There is an attitude running through the Australian poems of the bush that it is good and dignified to be clever, funny and an honest worker, but never the fop or dandy. The practical Spencer's creation of the ingenious McDougall is a good example of this ideal.

'IN RE A GENTLEMAN, ONE'

*When an attorney is called before the Full Court to answer for any alleged misconduct
it is not usual to publish his name until he is found guilty; until then the matter appears in the papers as
'In re a Gentleman, One of the Attorneys of the Supreme Court', or, more shortly, 'In re a Gent., One'.*

We see it each day in the paper,
   And know that there's mischief in store;
That some unprofessional caper
   Has landed a shark on the shore.
We know there'll be plenty of trouble
   Before they get through with the fun,
Because he's been coming the double
   On clients, has 'Gentleman, One'.

Alas for the gallant attorney,
   Intent upon cutting a dash!
He starts on life's perilous journey
   With rather more cunning than cash.
And fortune at first is inviting—
   He struts his brief hour in the sun—
But, lo! on the wall is the writing
   Of Nemesis, 'Gentleman, One'.

For soon he runs short of the dollars,
   He fears he must go to the wall;
So Peter's trust-money he collars
   To pay off his creditor, Paul;
Then robs right and left—for he goes it
   In earnest when once he's begun.
Descensus averni—he knows it;
   It's easy for 'Gentleman, One'.

The crash comes as sure as the seasons;
   He loses his coin in a mine,
Or booming in land, or for reasons
   Connected with women and wine.
Or maybe the cards or the horses
   A share of the damage have done—
No matter; the end of the course is
   The same: '*Re* a Gentleman, One,'

He struggles awhile to keep going,
   To stave off detection and shame;
But creditors, clamorous growing,
   Ere long put an end to the game.
At length the poor soldier of Satan
   His course to a finish has run—
And just think of Windeyer waiting
   To deal with 'A Gentleman, One'!

And some face it boldly, and brazen
   The shame and the utter disgrace;
While others, more sensitive, hasten
   Their names and their deeds to efface.
They snap the frail thread which the Furies
   And Fates have so cruelly spun.
May the great Final Judge and His juries
   Have mercy on 'Gentleman, One'!

A.B. PATERSON

THE DYING STOCKMAN

(Air—'The Old Stable Jacket')

A strapping young stockman lay dying,
His saddle supporting his head;
His two mates around him were crying,
As he rose on his elbow and said:

Chorus
'Wrap me up with my stockwhip and blanket,
And bury me deep down below,
Where the dingoes and crows can't molest me,
In the shade where the coolibahs grow.

'Oh! had I the flight of the bronzewing,
Far o'er the plains would I fly,
Straight to the land of my childhood,
And there I would lay down and die.

'Then cut down a couple of saplings,
Place one at my head and my toe,
Carve on them cross, stockwhip, and saddle,
To show there's a stockman below.

'Hark! there's the wail of a dingo,
Watchful and weird—I must go,
For it tolls the death-knell of the stockman
From the gloom of the scrub down below.

'There's tea in the battered old billy;
Place the pannikins out in a row,
And we'll drink to the next merry meeting,
In the place where all good fellows go.

'And oft in the shades of the twilight,
When the soft winds are whispering low,
And the darkening shadows are falling,
Sometimes think of the stockman below.'

ANON

WHEN THE TEAMS BROUGHT IN THE WOOL

I loaded at George Elbourne's some thirty bales of wool
And went across the Junction and I never got a pull
Till I came to the end of the logging when I gave the whip a crack
And I dropped down to the axle in one of Western's tracks.

Then Scabby Tommy came along to have a blooming look
And said, 'If you don't slew them round you'll have them in the muck';
We slewed them to the near side as it was the hardest ground,
And while I flew the jingler old Violet ran aground.

We slewed them to the off side to give them another try,
And just as we were starting them old Six Mile Bill come by;
He said, 'You'll have to dig her, else you'll never get her out,'
And you can bet old Six Mile Bill he knows what he's about.

Old Six Mile Bill he got a stick to dig away the muck
And it took a lot of digging to liberate the 'truck';
Then journeyed straight 'way on to Kemp's, just seven miles from here,
Where Tommy he drank whisky and Barney he drank beer.

We stopped there for an hour or so and drank just what was right,
And Tommy he came round in front and said, 'Old Kemp I'll fight.'
We hurried on to Pittsworth as we had the wool to truck,
Then had a drink or two in town, and Barn' fought Shuttlebuck.

But Shuttlebuck he licked him, as you can plainly hear,
But Barney said, ''Twas not his fault, 'twas Johnny Barrett's beer.'
In those days life was a pleasure, no man was known to frown,
He simply took the good with the bad, and brought the wool-clip down.

BARNEY O'TOOLE

THE BULLETIN HOTEL

I was drifting in the drizzle past the Cecil in the Strand—
Which, I'm told, is very tony—and its front looks very grand;
And I somehow fell a-thinking of a pub I know so well,
Of a palace in Australia called The Bulletin Hotel.

Just a little six-room'd shanty built of corrugated tin,
And all round a blazing desert—land of camels, thirst and sin;
And the landlord is 'the Spider'—Western diggers know him well—
Charlie Webb!—Ah, there you have it!—of the Bulletin Hotel.

'Tis a big soft-hearted spider in a land where life is grim,
And a web of great good-nature that brings worn-out flies to him:
'Tis the club of many lost souls in the wide Westralian hell,
And the stage of many Mitchells is the Bulletin Hotel.

But the swagman, on his uppers, pulls an undertaker's mug,
And he leans across the counter and he breathes in Charlie's lug—
Tale of thirst and of misfortune. Charlie knows it, and—ah, well!
But it's very bad for business at the Bulletin Hotel.

'What's a drink or two?' says Charlie, 'and you can't refuse a feed';
But there's many a drink unpaid for, many sticks of 'borrowed' weed;
And the poor old spineless bummer and the broken-hearted swell
Know that they are sure of tucker at the Bulletin Hotel.

There's the liquor and the license and the 'carriage' and the rent,
And the sea or grave 'twixt Charlie and the fivers he has lent;
And I'm forced to think in sorrow, for I know the country well,
That the end will be the bailiff in the Bulletin Hotel.

But he'll pack up in a hurry and he'll seek a cooler clime,
If I make a rise in England and I get out there in time.
For a mate o' mine is Charlie and I stayed there for a spell,
And I owe more than a jingle to the Bulletin Hotel.

But there's lots of graft between us, there are many miles of sea,
So, if you should drop in on Charlie, just shake hands with him for me;
Say I think the Bush less lonely than the great town where I dwell,
And—a grander than the Cecil is the Bulletin Hotel.

HENRY LAWSON

LAY OF THE MOTOR CAR

We're away! and the wind whistles shrewd
    In our whiskers and teeth;
And the granite-like grey of the road
    Seems to slide underneath.
As an eagle might sweep through the sky,
    So we sweep through the land;
And the pallid pedestrians fly
    When they hear us at hand.

We outpace, we outlast, we outstrip!
    Not the fast-fleeing hare,
Nor the racehorses under the whip,
    Nor the birds of the air
Can compete with our swiftness sublime,
    Our ease and our grace.
We annihilate chickens and time
    And policemen and space.

Do you mind that fat grocer who crossed?
    How he dropped down to pray
In the road when he saw he was lost;
    How he melted away
Underneath, and there rang through the fog
    His earsplitting squeal
As he went—Is that he or a dog,
    That stuff on the wheel?

A.B. Paterson

BELL-BIRDS

By channels of coolness the echoes are calling,
And down the dim gorges I hear the creek falling:
It lives in the mountain where moss and the sedges
Touch with their beauty the banks and the ledges.
Through breaks of the cedar and sycamore bowers
Struggles the light that is love to the flowers;
And, softer than slumber, and sweeter than singing,
The notes of the bell-birds are running and ringing.

The silver-voiced bell-birds, the darlings of daytime!
They sing in September their songs of the May-time;
When shadows wax strong, and the thunder-bolts hurtle,
They hide with their fear in the leaves of the myrtle;
When rain and the sunbeams shine mingled together,
They start up like fairies that follow fair weather;
And straightway the hues of their feathers unfolden
Are the green and the purple, the blue and the golden.

October, the maiden of bright yellow tresses,
Loiters for love in these cool wildernesses;
Loiters, knee-deep, in the grasses, to listen,
Where dripping rocks gleam and the leafy pools glisten:
Then is the time when the water-moons splendid
Break with their gold, and are scattered or blended
Over the creeks, till the woodlands have warning
Of songs of the bell-bird and wings of the Morning.

Welcome as waters unkissed by the summers
Are the voices of bell-birds to thirsty far-comers.
When fiery December sets foot in the forest,
And the need of the wayfarer presses the sorest,
Pent in the ridges for ever and ever
The bell-birds direct him to spring and to river,
With ring and with ripple, like runnels whose torrents
Are toned by the pebbles and leaves in the currents.

Often I sit, looking back to a childhood,
Mixt with the sights and the sounds of the wildwood,
Longing for power and the sweetness to fashion
Lyrics with beats like the heart-beats of Passion;—
Songs interwoven of lights and of laughters
Borrowed from bell-birds in far forest-rafters;
So I might keep in the city and alleys
The beauty and strength of the deep mountain valleys:
Charming to slumber the pain of my losses
With glimpses of creeks and a vision of mosses.

HENRY KENDALL

FROM THE GULF

Store cattle from Nelanjie! The mob goes feeding past,
With half a mile of sandhill 'twixt the leaders and the last;
The nags that move behind them are the good old
   Queensland stamp—
Short backs and perfect shoulders that are priceless on a camp;
And these are *Men* that ride them, broad-chested, tanned, and tall,
The bravest hearts amongst us and the lightest hands of all;
Oh, let them wade in Wonga grass and taste the Wonga dew,
And let them spread, those thousand head—for we've
   been droving too!

Store cattle from Nelanjie! By half a hundred towns,
By Northern ranges rough and red, by rolling open downs,
By stock-routes brown and burnt and bare, by flood —
   wrapped river-bends,
They've hunted them from gate to gate—the drover has no friends!
But idly they may ride today beneath the scorching sun
And let the hungry bullocks try the grass on Wonga run;
No overseer will dog them here to 'see the cattle through',
But they may spread their thousand head—for we've been
   droving too!

Store cattle from Nelanjie! They've a naked track to steer;
The stockyards at Wodonga are a long way down from here;
The creeks won't run till God knows when, and half the
   holes are dry;
The tanks are few and far between and water's dear to buy;
There's plenty at the Brolga bore for all his stock andmine—
We'll pass him with a brave God-speed across the Border Line;
And if he goes a five-mile stage and loiters slowly through,
We'll only think the more of him—for we've been droving too!

Store cattle from Nelanjie! They're mute as milkers now;
But yonder grizzled drover, with the care-lines on his brow,
Could tell of merry musters on the big Nelanjie plains,
With blood upon the chestnut's flanks and foam upon the reins;
Could tell of nights upon the road when those same mild-eyed steers
Went ringing round the river bend and through the scrub like spears;
And if his words are rude and rough, we know his words are true,
We know what wild Nelanjies are—and we've been droving too!

Store cattle from Nelanjie! Around the fire at night
They've watched the pine-tree shadows lift before the dancing light;
They've lain awake to listen when the weird bush-voices speak,
And heard the lilting bells go by along the empty creek;
They've spun the yarns of hut and camp, the tales of play and work,
The wondrous tales that gild the road from Normanton to Bourke;
They've told of fortune foul and fair, of women false and true,
And well we know the songs they've sung—for we've
   been droving too!

Store cattle from Nelanjie! Their breath is on the breeze;
You hear them tread, a thousand head, in blue-grass to the knees;
The lead is on the netting-fence, the wings are spreading wide,
The lame and laggard scarcely move—so slow the drovers ride!
But let them stay and feed today for sake of Auld Lang Syne;
They'll never get a chance like this below the Border Line;
And if they tread our frontage down, what's that to me or you?
What's ours to fare, by God they'll share! For we've been droving too!

WILL H. OGILVIE

THE DROVERS

Shrivelled leather, rusty buckles, and the rot is in our knuckles,
Scorched for months upon the pommel while the brittle rein hung free;
Shrunken eyes that once were lighted with fresh boyhood, dull and blighted—
And the sores upon our eyelids are unpleasant sights to see.
And our hair is thin and dying from the ends, with too long lying
In the night dews on the ashes of the Dry Countree.

Yes, we've seen 'em 'bleaching whitely' where the salt-bush sparkles brightly,
But their grins were over-friendly, so we passed and let them be.
And we've seen them 'rather recent', and we've stopped to hide 'em decent
When they weren't nice to handle and they weren't too nice to see;
We have heard the dry bones rattle under fifteen hundred cattle—
Seen the rags go up in dust-clouds and the brittle joints kicked free;
But there's little time to tarry, if you wish to live and marry,
When the cattle shy at something in the Dry Countree.

No, you needn't fear the blacks on the Never Never tracks—
For the Myall in his freedom's an uncommon sight to see;
Oh! we do not stick at trifles—and the trackers sneak their rifles,
And go strolling in the gloaming while the sergeant's yarning free:
Round the Myalls creep the trackers—there's a sound like firing crackers
And—the blacks are getting scarcer in the Dry Countree
(Goes an unprotected maiden 'cross the clearing carrion-laden—
Oh, they ride 'em down on horseback in the Dry Countree).

But you don't know what might happen when a tank is but a trap on.
Roofs of hell, and there is nothing but the blaze of hell to see:
And the phantom water's lapping—and no limb for saddle-strapping—
Better carry your revolver through the Dry Countree.
But I'm feeling gay and frisky, come with me and have a whisky!
Change of hells is all we live for (that's my mate that's got D.T.):
We have fought through hell's own weather, he and I and death together—
Oh, the devil grins to greet us from the Dry Countree!

HENRY LAWSON

THEY MET IN THE HALL AT A CHARITY BALL

They met in the hall, at a Charity Ball,
    Patronised by the pink of Society,
They were both in a state, I grieve to relate,
    That the Clergyman calls insobriety.

He wanted to know was she *comme il faut,*
    Or whether her manner was shadylike,
And he wondered in doubt, as she lowered a stout,
    In a style more proficient than ladylike.

He asked might he call, the night after the Ball,
If she'd pardon his impetuosity,
She embraced him and said, 'You must come home to bed,
Just to show there is no animosity.'

She sang him a song, as they rattled along,
    There were verses a little bit blue in it,
And a story she told of adventures of old,
With a queer situation or two in it.

When they went to repose, and he threw off his clothes,
    In his anxious excitement to doss it, he
Was knocked when she bid him fork out two quid,
    Just to show there was no animosity.

'Twas a little bit rough, but he forked out the stuff,
    Though he thought it was very absurd of her,
Then she went down below, for a moment or so,
    And that was the last that he heard of her.

For a big-shouldered lout came and lumbered him out,
    And used him with awful ferocity,
He was very much hurt, but they chucked him his shirt,
    Just to show there was no animosity.

A.B. PATERSON

THE ROAD TO HOGAN'S GAP

Now look, y' see, it's this way like,
  Y' cross the broken bridge
And run the crick down till y' strike
  The second right-hand ridge.

The track is hard to see in parts,
  But still it's pretty clear;
There's been two Injin hawkers' carts
  Along that road this year.

Well, run that right-hand ridge along,
  It ain't, to say, too steep.
There's two fresh tracks might put y' wrong
  Where blokes went out with sheep.

But keep the crick upon your right,
  And follow pretty straight
Along the spur, until y' sight
  A wire and sapling gate.

Well, that's where Hogan's old grey mare
  Fell off and broke her back;
You'll see her carcase layin' there,
  Jist down below the track.

And then you drop two mile, or three,
  It's pretty steep and blind;
You want to go and fall a tree
  And tie it on behind.

And then you'll pass a broken cart
  Below a granite bluff;
And that is where you strike the part
  They reckon pretty rough.

But by the time you've got that far
  It's either cure or kill,
So turn your horses round the spur
  And face 'em up the hill.

For, look, if you should miss the slope
  And get below the track,
You haven't got the whitest hope
  Of ever gettin' back.

An' halfway up you'll see the hide
  Of Hogan's brindled bull;
Well, mind and keep the right-hand side,
  The left's too steep a pull.

And both the banks is full of cracks;
  An' just about at dark
You'll see the last year's bullock tracks
  Where Hogan drew the bark.

The marks is old and pretty faint
  And grown with scrub and such;
Of course the track to Hogan's ain't
  A road that's travelled much.

But turn and run the tracks along
  For half a mile or more,
And then, of course, you can't go wrong—
  You're right at Hogan's door.

When first you come to Hogan's gate
  He mightn't show, perhaps;
He's pretty sure to plant and wait
  To see it ain't the traps.

I wouldn't call it good enough
  To let your horses out;
There's some that's pretty extra rough
  Is livin' round about.

It's likely if your horses did
  Get feedin' near the track,
It's goin' to cost at least a quid
  Or more to get them back.

So, if you find they're off the place,
  It's up to you to go
And flash a quid in Hogan's face—
  He'll know the blokes that know.

But, listen, if you're feelin' dry,
  Just see there's no one near,
And go and wink the other eye
  And ask for ginger beer.

The blokes come in from near and far
  To sample Hogan's pop;
They reckon once they breast the bar
  They stay there till they drop.

On Sundays you can see them spread
  Like flies around the tap.
It's like that song 'The Livin' Dead'
  Up there at Hogan's Gap.

They like to make it pretty strong
   Whenever there's a charnce;
So when a stranger comes along
   They always holds a darnce.

There's recitations, songs, and fights,
   They do the thing a treat.
There's one long bloke up there recites
   As well as e'er you'd meet.

They're lively blokes all right up there,
   It's never dull a day.
I'd go meself if I could spare
   The time to get away.

The stranger turned his horses, quick,
   He didn't cross the bridge.
He didn't go along the crick
   To strike the second ridge.

He didn't make the trip, because
   He wasn't feeling fit.
His business up at Hogan's was
   To serve him with a writ.

He reckoned if he faced the pull
   And climbed the rocky stair,
The next to come might find his hide
A landmark on the mountain side,
Along with Hogan's brindled bull
   And Hogan's old grey mare!

A.B. PATERSON

27

THE TEAMS

A cloud of dust on the long white road,
And the teams go creeping on
Inch by inch with the weary load;
And by the power of the greenhide goad
The distant goal is won.

With eyes half-shut to the blinding dust,
And necks to the yokes bent low,
The beasts are pulling as bullocks must;
And the shining tyres might almost rust
While the spokes are turning slow.

With face half-hid 'neath a broad-brimmed hat
That shades from the heat's white waves,
And shouldered whip with its greenhide plait,
The driver plods with a gait like that
Of his weary, patient slaves.

He wipes his brow, for the day is hot,
And spits to the left with spite;
He shouts at 'Bally', and flicks at 'Scot',
And raises dust from the back of 'Spot',
And spits to the dusty right.

He'll sometimes pause as a thing of form
In front of a settler's door,
And ask for a drink, and remark, 'It's warm,'
Or say, 'There's signs of a thunderstorm';
But he seldom utters more.

But the rains are heavy on roads like these;
And, fronting his lonely home,
For weeks together the settler sees
The teams bogged down to the axletrees,
Or ploughing the sodden loam.

And then when the roads are at their worst,
The bushman's children hear
The cruel blows of the whips reversed
While bullocks pull as their hearts would burst,
And bellow with pain and fear.

And thus with little joy or rest
Are the long, long journeys done;
And thus—'tis a cruel war at the best—
Is distance fought in the mighty West,
And the lonely battles won.

HENRY LAWSON

THE BUSH FIRE

Ah, better the thud of the deadly gun, and the crash of the bursting shell,
Than the terrible silence where drought is fought out there in the western hell;
And better the rattle of rifles near, or the thunder on deck at sea,
Than the sound—most hellish of all to hear—of a fire where it should not be.

On the runs to the west of the Dingo Scrubs there was drought, and ruin, and death,
And the sandstorm came from the dread north-east with the blast of a furnace-breath;
Till at last one day, at the fierce sunrise, a boundary-rider woke,
And saw, in the place of the distant haze, a curtain of light blue smoke.

There is saddling-up by the cockey's hut, and out in the station yard,
And away to the north, north-east, north-west, the bushmen are riding hard.
The pickets are out and many a scout, and many a mulga wire,
While Bill and Jim, with their faces grim, are riding to meet the fire.

It roars for days in the hopeless scrubs, and across, where the ground seems bare,
With a cackle and hiss, like the hissing of snakes, the fire is travelling there;
Till at last, exhausted by sleeplessness, and the terrible toil and heat,
The squatter is crying, 'My God! the wool!' and the farmer, 'My God! the wheat!'

But there comes a drunkard (who reels as he rides), with the news from the roadside pub:
'Pat Murphy —the cockey—cut off by the fire!—way back in the Dingo Scrub!
Let the wheat and the woolshed go to—' Well, they do as each great heart bids;
They are riding a race for the Dingo Scrub—for Pat and his wife and kids.

And who is leading the race with death? An ill matched three, you'll allow;
Flash Jim the breaker and Boozing Bill (who is riding steadily now),
And Constable Dunn, of the Mounted Police, is riding between the two
(He wants Flash Jim, but the job can wait till they get the Murphys through).

As they strike the track through the blazing scrub, the trooper is heard to shout:
'We'll take them on to the Two-mile Tank, if we cannot bring them out!'
A half mile more, and the rest rein back, retreating, half-choked, half-blind;
And the three are gone from the sight of men, and the bush fire roars behind.

The Bushman wiped the tears of smoke, and like Bushmen wept and swore;
'Poor Bill will be wanting his drink to-night as never he did before.'
'And Dunn was the best in the whole damned force!' says a client of Dunn's, with pride;
I reckon he'll serve his summons on Jim—when they get to the other side.

It is daylight again, and the fire is past, and the black scrub silent and grim,
Except for the blaze of an old dead tree, or the crash of a falling limb;
And the Bushmen are riding again on the run, with hearts and with eyes that fill,
To look for the bodies of Constable Dunn, Flash Jim, and Boozing Bill.

They are found in the mud of the Two-mile Tank, where a fiend might scarce survive,
But the Bushmen gather from words they hear that the bodies are much alive.
There is Swearing Pat, with his grey beard singed, and his language of lurid hue,
And his tough old wife, and his half-baked kids, and the three who dragged them through.

Old Pat is deploring his burnt-out home, and his wife the climate warm;
And Jim the loss of his favourite horse, and Dunn his uniform;
And Boozing Bill, with a raging thirst, is cursing the Dingo Scrub—
He'll only ask for the loan of a flask and a lift to the nearest pub.

Flash Jim the Breaker is lying low—blue-paper is after him,
And Dunn, the trooper, is riding his rounds with a blind eye out for Jim,
And Boozing Bill is fighting D.T.'s in the township of Sudden Jerk—
When they're wanted again in the Dingo Scrubs, they'll be there to do the work.

HENRY LAWSON

THE WILD COLONIAL BOY

There was a wild colonial boy, Jack Donahoe by name,
Of poor but honest parents he was born in Castlemaine.
He was his father's dearest hope, his mother's pride and joy.
O, fondly did his parents love their Wild Colonial Boy.

Chorus
So ride with me, my hearties, we'll cross the mountains high.
Together we will plunder, together we will die.
We'll wander through the valleys and gallop o'er the plains,
For scorn we to live in slavery, bound down with iron chains!

He was scarcely sixteen years of age when he left his father's home,
A convict to Australia, across the seas to roam.
They put him in the Iron Gang in the Government employ,
But ne'er an iron on earth could hold the Wild Colonial Boy.

And when they sentenced him to hang to end his wild career,
With a shout of defiance bold Donahoe broke clear.
He robbed those wealthy squatters, their stock he did destroy,
But never a trap in the land could catch the Wild Colonial Boy.

Then one day when he was cruising near the broad Nepean's side,
From out the thick Bringelly bush the horse police did ride.
'Die or resign, Jack Donahoe!' they shouted in their joy.
'I'll fight this night with all my might!' cried the Wild Colonial Boy.

He fought six rounds with the horse police before the fatal ball,
Which pierced his heart with cruel smart, caused Donahoe to fall.
And then he closed his mournful eyes, his pistol an empty toy,
Crying: 'Parents dear, O say a prayer for the Wild Colonial Boy.'

ANON

IT'S GRAND

It's grand to be a squatter
 And sit upon a post,
And watch your little ewes and lambs
 A-giving up the ghost.

It's grand to be a 'cockie'
 With wife and kids to keep,
And find an all-wise Providence
 Has mustered all your sheep.

It's grand to be a Western man,
 With shovel in your hand,
To dig your little homestead out
 From underneath the sand.

It's grand to be a shearer,
 Along the Darling side,
And pluck the wool from stinking sheep
 That some days since have died.

It's grand to be a rabbit
 And breed till all is blue,
And then to die in heaps because
 There's nothing left to chew.

It's grand to be a Minister
 And travel like a swell,
And tell the Central District folk
 To go to—Inverell.

It's grand to be a Socialist
 And lead the bold array
That marches to prosperity
 At seven bob a day.

It's grand to be an unemployed
 And lie in the Domain,
And wake up every second day
 And go to sleep again.

It's grand to borrow English tin
 To pay for wharves and Rocks,
And then to find it isn't in
 The little money-box.

It's grand to be a democrat
 And toady to the mob,
For fear that if you told the truth
 They'd hunt you from your job.

It's grand to be a lot of things
 In this fair Southern land,
But if the Lord would send us rain,
 That would, indeed, be grand!

A.B. PATERSON

34

THOSE NAMES

The shearers sat in the firelight, hearty and hale and strong
After the hard day's shearing, passing the joke along:
The 'ringer' that shore a hundred, as they never were shorn before,
And the novice who, toiling bravely, had tommy-hawked half a score,
The tarboy, the cook, and the slushy, the sweeper that swept the board,
The picker-up, and the penner, with the rest of the shearing horde.
There were men from the inland stations where the skies like a furnace glow,
And men from the Snowy River, the land of the frozen snow;
There were swarthy Queensland drovers who reckoned all land by miles,
And farmers' sons from the Murray, where many a vineyard smiles.
They started at telling stories when they wearied of cards and games,
And to give these stories a flavour they threw in some local names,
And a man from the bleak Monaro, away on the tableland,
He fixed his eyes on the ceiling, and he started to play his hand.

He told them of Adjintoothbong, where the pine-clad mountains freeze,
And the weight of the snow in summer breaks branches off the trees,
And, as he warmed to the business, he let them have it strong—
Nimitybelle, Conargo, Wheeo, Bongongolong;
He lingered over them fondly, because they recalled to mind
A thought of the old bush homestead, and the girl that he left behind.
Then the shearers all sat silent till a man in the corner rose;
Said he, 'I've travelled a-plenty but never heard names like those,
Out in the western districts, out on the Castlereagh
Most of the names are easy—short for a man to say.
You've heard of Mungrybambone and the Gundabluey pine,
Quobbotha, Girilambone, and Terramungamine,
Quambone, Eunonyhareenyha, Wee Waa, and Buntijo—'
But the rest of the shearers stopped him: 'For the sake of your jaw, go slow,
If you reckon those names are short ones out where such names prevail,
Just try and remember some long ones before you begin the tale.'

And the man from the western district, though never a word he said,
Just winked with his dexter eyelid, and then he retired to bed.

A.B. PATERSON

SUNRISE ON THE COAST

Grey dawn on the sand-hills—the night wind has drifted
    All night from the rollers a scent of the sea;
With the dawn the grey fog his battalions has lifted,
    At the call of the morning they scatter and flee.

Like mariners calling the roll of their number
    The sea-fowl put out to the infinite deep.
And far overhead—sinking softly to slumber—
    Worn out by their watching the stars fall asleep.

To eastward, where rests the broad dome of the skies on
    The sea-line, stirs softly the curtain of night;
And far from behind the enshrouded horizon
    Comes the voice of a God saying 'Let there be light.'

And lo, there is light! Evanescent and tender,
    It glows ruby-red where 'twas now ashen-grey;
And purple and scarlet and gold in its splendour—
    Behold, 'tis that marvel, the birth of a day!

A.B. PATERSON

WHEAT

'Sowin' things an' growin' things, an' watchin' of 'em grow;
That's the game,' my father said, an' father ought to know.
'Settin' things an' gettin' things to grow for folks to eat:
That's life,' my father said, 'That's very hard to beat.'
For my father was a farmer, as his father was before,
Just sowin' things an' growin' things in far-off days of yore,
In the far-off land of England, till my father found his feet
In the new land, in the true land, where he took to growin' wheat.
   Wheat, Wheat, Wheat! Oh, the sound of it is sweet!
   I've been praisin' it an' raisin' it in rain an' wind an' heat
     Since the time I learned to toddle, till it's beatin' in my noddle,
   Is the little song I'm singin' you of Wheat, Wheat, Wheat.

Plantin' things—an' grantin' things is goin' as they should,
An' the weather altogether is behavin' pretty good—
Is a pleasure in a measure for a man that likes the game,
An' my father he would rather raise a crop than make a name,
For my father was a farmer, an' 'All fame,' he said, 'ain't reel;
An' the same it isn't fillin' when you're wantin' for a meal.'
So I'm followin' his footsteps, an' a-keepin' of my feet,
While I cater for the nation with my Wheat, Wheat, Wheat.
   Wheat, Wheat, Wheat! When the poets all are beat
   By the reason that the season for the verse crop is a cheat,
     Then I comes up bright an' grinnin' with the knowledge that I'm
       winnin',
   With the rhythm of my harvester an' Wheat, Wheat, Wheat.

Readin' things an' heedin' things that clever fellers give,
An' ponderin' an' wonderin' why we was meant to live—
Muddlin' through an' fuddlin' through philosophy an' such
Is a game I never took to, an' it doesn't matter much.
For my father was a farmer, as I might 'a' said before,
An' the sum of his philosophy was, 'Grow a little more.
For growin' things,' my father said, 'it makes life sort o' sweet
An' your conscience never swats you if your game is
   growin' wheat.'
   Wheat, Wheat, Wheat! Oh, the people have to eat!
   An' you're servin', an' deservin' of a velvet-cushion seat
     In the cocky-farmers' heaven when you come to throw a seven;
   An' your password at the portal will be, 'Wheat, Wheat, Wheat.'

Now, the preacher an' the teacher have a callin' that is high
While they're spoutin' to the doubtin' of the happy by an' by;
But I'm sayin' that the prayin' it is better for their souls
When they've plenty wheat inside 'em in the shape of penny rolls.
For my father was a farmer, an' he used to sit an' grieve
When he thought about the apple that old Adam got from Eve.
It was foolin' with an orchard where the serpent got 'em beat,
An' they might 'a' kept the homestead if they'd simply stuck to wheat.
   Wheat, Wheat, Wheat! If you're seekin' to defeat
   Care an' worry in the hurry of the crowded city street,
     Leave the hustle all behind you; come an' let contentment find you
   In a cosy little cabin lyin' snug among the wheat.

In the city, more's the pity, thousands live an' thousands die
Never carin', never sparin' pains that fruits may multiply;
Breathin', livin', never givin'; greedy but to have an' take,
Dyin' with no day behind 'em lived for fellow-mortals' sake.
Now my father was a farmer, an' he used to sit and laugh
At the 'fools o' life', he called 'em, livin' on the other half.
Dyin' lonely, missin' only that one joy that makes live sweet—
Just the joy of useful labour, such as comes of growin' wheat.
   Wheat, Wheat, Wheat! Let the foolish scheme an' cheat;
   But I'd rather, like my father, when my span o' life's complete,
     Feel I'd lived by helpin' others; earned the right to call 'em brothers
   Who had gained while I was gainin' from God's earth His gift of wheat.

When the settin' sun is gettin' low above the western hills,
When the creepin' shadows deepen, and a peace the whole land fills,
Then I often sort o' soften with a feelin' like content,
An' I feel like thankin' Heaven for a day in labour spent.
For my father was a farmer, an' he used to sit an' smile,
Realisin' he was wealthy in what makes a life worth while.
Smilin', he has told me often, 'After all the toil an' heat,
Lad, he's paid in more than silver who has grown one field of wheat.'
   Wheat, Wheat, Wheat! When it comes my turn to meet
   Death the Reaper, an' the Keeper of the Judgement Book I greet,
     Then I'll face 'em sort o' calmer with the solace of the farmer,
   That he's fed a million brothers with his Wheat, Wheat, Wheat.

C.J. DENNIS

LAMBED DOWN

(Air—'Excelsior')

The shades of night were falling fast,
As down a steep old gully passed
A man whom you could plainly see
Had just come off a drunken spree,
   Lambed down.

He'd left the station with his cheque,
And little evil did he reck;
At Ryan's pub he felt all right,
And yet he was, before the night,
   Lambed down.

'Oh, stay!' old Ryan said, 'and slip
Your blanket off, and have a nip;
I'll cash your cheque and send you on.'
He stopped and now his money's gone—
   Lambed down.

He's got the shakes and think he sees
Blue devils lurking in the trees;
Oh, shearers! if you've any sense
Don't be on any such pretence
   Lambed down.

ANON

THE SWAGMAN AND HIS MATE

From north to south throughout the year
The shearing seasons run,
The Queensland stations start to shear
When Maoriland has done;
But labour's cheap and runs are wide,
And some the track must tread
From New Year's Day till Christmastide
And never get a shed!
North, west, and south—south, west, and north—
They lead and follow Fate—
The stoutest hearts that venture forth—
The swagman and his mate.

A restless, homeless class they are
Who tramp in border land.
They take their rest 'neath moon and star—
Their bed the desert sand,
On sunset tracks they ride and tramp,
Till speech has almost died,
And still they drift from camp to camp
In silence side by side.
They think and dream, as all men do;
Perchance their dreams are great—
Each other's thoughts are sacred to
The swagman and his mate.

With scrubs beneath the stifling skies
Unstirred by heaven's breath;
Beyond the Darling Timber lies
The land of living death!
A land that wrong-born poets brave
Till dulled minds cease to grope—
A land where all things perish, save
The memories of Hope.
When daylight's fingers point out back
(And seem to hesitate)
The far faint dust cloud marks their track—
The swagman and his mate.

And one who followed through the scrub
And out across the plain,
And only in a bitter mood
Would see those tracks again;—
Can only write what he has seen—
Can only give his hand—
And greet those mates in words that mean
'I know', 'I understand'.
I hope they'll find the squatter 'white',
The cook and shearers 'straight',
When they have reached the shed to-night—
The swagman and his mate.

HENRY LAWSON

NORTHWARDS TO THE SHEDS

There's a whisper from the regions out beyond the Barwon banks;
There's a gathering of the legions and a forming of the ranks;
There's a murmur coming nearer with the signs that never fail,
And it's time for every shearer to be out upon the trail.
They must leave their girls behind them and their empty glasses too,
For there's plenty left to mind them when they cross the dry Barcoo;
There'll be kissing, there'll be sorrow such as only sweethearts know,
But before the noon to-morrow they'll be singing as they go—

> *For the Western creeks are calling,*
> *And the idle days are done,*
> *With the snowy fleeces falling*
> *And the Queensland sheds begun!*

There is shortening of the bridle, there is tightening of the girth,
There is fondling of the idol that they love the best on earth;
Northward from the Lachlan River and the sun-dried Castlereagh,
Outward to the Never-Never ride the ringers on their way.
From the green bends of the Murray they have run their horses in,
For there's haste and there is hurry when the Queensland sheds begin;
On the Bogan they are bridling, they are saddling on the Bland;
There is plunging and there's sidling—for the colts don't understand

> *That the Western creeks are calling,*
> *And the idle days are done,*
> *With the snowy fleeces falling*
> *And the Queensland sheds begun!*

They will camp below the station, they'll be cutting peg and pole,
Rearing tents for occupation till the calling of the roll;
And it's time the nags were driven, and it's time to strap the pack,
For there's never licence given to the laggards on the track.
Hark the music of the battle! It is time to bare our swords;
Do you hear the rush and rattle as they tramp along the boards?
They are past the pen-doors picking light-light-woolled weaners one by one;
I can hear the shear-blades clicking and now I know the fight's begun!

WILL H. OGILVIE

THE LAST MUSTER

All day we had driven the starving sheep to the scrub
    where the axes ply,
And the weakest had lagged upon weary feet and
    dropped from the ranks to die;
And the crows flew up from the rotting heaps and the
    ewes too weak to stand,
And the fences flaunted red skins like flags, and the dour
    drought held the land.

And at night as I lay a-dreaming, I woke, and a silver moon
Shone fair on a dancing river and laughed to a broad lagoon,
And the grass turned over the fences and rippled like
    ripening grain,
And clouds hung low on the hilltops, and earth smelt
    sweet with the rain.

And in at the open window the lowing of cattle came—
A mob that had never a laggard and never a beast that
    was lame;
And wethers, a thousand thousand, and ewes with their
    lambs beside,
Moved over the green flats feeding, spread river to ranges
    wide.

And horses whinnied below me, and leaning I watched
    them pass,
Lusty and strong and playful like horses on spring-tide grass
When they whinny one to another, strong-voiced, and a
    gallop brings
Foam to the flank, be it only from paddock to stockyard
    wings.

Slowly they moved in the moon-mist, heads low in the
    cool night-dew,
Snatching the long bush grasses, breast-high as they
    wandered through;
Slowly they moved in the moon-mist, and never a horse
    on the plains
Was red with the gall of the collar or marked with a
    chafe of the chains.

And behind them a hundred drovers rode slow on their
    horses white,
All brave with their trappings of silver that flashed in the
    silver light;
Buckle and stirrup and bridle, and spurs for their better
    speed—
Singing behind the cattle like drovers on royal feed.

WILL H. OGILVIE

SONG OF THE ARTESIAN WATER

Now the stock have started dying, for the Lord has sent a drought;
But we're sick of prayers and Providence—we're going to do without;
With the derricks up above us and the solid earth below,
We are waiting at the lever for the word to let her go.
    Sinking down, deeper down,
    Oh, we'll sink it deeper down:
As the drill is plugging downward at a thousand feet of level,
If the Lord won't send us water, oh, we'll get it from the devil;
Yes, we'll get it from the devil deeper down.

Now, our engine's built in Glasgow by a very canny Scot,
And he marked it twenty horse-power, but he don't know what is what:
When Canadian Bill is firing with the sun-dried gidgee logs,
She can equal thirty horses and a score or so of dogs.
    Sinking down, deeper down,
    Oh, we're going deeper down:
If we fail to get the water then it's ruin to the squatter,
For the drought is on the station and the weather's growing hotter,
But we're bound to get the water deeper down.

But the shaft has started caving and the sinking's very slow,
And the yellow rods are bending in the water down below,
And the tubes are always jamming and they can't be made to shift
Till we nearly burst the engine with a forty horse-power lift.
    Sinking down, deeper down,
    Oh, we're going deeper down:
Though the shaft is always caving, and the tubes are always jamming,
Yet we'll fight our way to water while the stubborn drill is ramming—
While the stubborn drill is ramming deeper down.

But there's no artesian water, though we've passed three thousand feet,
And the contract price is growing and the boss is nearly beat.
But it must be down beneath us, and it's down we've got to go,
Though she's bumping on the solid rock four thousand feet below.
    Sinking down, deeper down,
    Oh, we're going deeper down:
And it's time they heard us knocking on the roof of Satan's dwellin';
But we'll get artesian water if we cave the roof of hell in—
Oh! we'll get artesian water deeper down.

But it's hark! the whistle's blowing with a wild, exultant blast,
And the boys are madly cheering, for they've struck the flow at last,
And it's rushing up the tubing from four thousand feet below
Till it spouts above the casing in a million-gallon flow.
    And it's down, deeper down,
    Oh, it comes from deeper down;
It is flowing, ever flowing, in a free, unstinted measure
From the silent hidden places where the old earth hides her treasure—
Where the old earth hides her treasure deeper down.

And it's clear away the timber, and it's let the water run:
How it glimmers in the shadow, how it flashes in the sun!
By the silent belts of timber, by the miles of blazing plain
It is bringing hope and comfort to the thirsty land again.
    Flowing down, further down;
    It is flowing further down
To the tortured thirsty cattle, bringing gladness in its going;
Through the droughty days of summer it is flowing, ever flowing—
It is flowing, ever flowing, further down.

A.B. PATERSON

ANDY'S RETURN

With pannikins all rusty,
And billy burnt and black,
And clothes all torn and dusty,
That scarcely hide his back;
With sun-cracked saddle-leather,
And knotted greenhide rein,
And face burnt brown with weather,
Our Andy's home again!

His unkempt hair is faded
With sleeping in the wet,
He's looking old and jaded;
But he is hearty yet.
With eyes sunk in their sockets—
But merry as of yore;
With big cheques in his pockets,
Our Andy's home once more!

Old Uncle's bright and cheerful;
He wears a smiling face;
And Aunty's never tearful
Now Andy's round the place.

Old Blucher barks for gladness;
He broke his rusty chain,
And leapt in joyous madness
When Andy came again.

With tales of flood and famine,
On distant northern tracks,
And shady yarns—'baal gammon!'
Of dealings with the blacks,
From where the skies hang lazy
On many a northern plain,
From regions dim and hazy
Our Andy's home again!

His toil is nearly over;
He'll soon enjoy his gains.
Not long he'll be a drover,
And cross the lonely plains.
We'll happy be for ever
When he'll no longer roam,
But by some deep, cool river
Will make us all a home.

HENRY LAWSON

THE WOMEN OF THE WEST

They left the vine-wreathed cottage and the mansion on the hill,
The houses in the busy streets where life is never still,
The pleasures of the city, and the friends they cherished best:
For love they faced the wilderness—the Women of the West.

The roar, and rush, and fever of the city died away,
And the old-time joys and faces—they were gone for many a day;
In their place the lurching coach-wheel, or the creaking bullock chains,
O'er the everlasting sameness of the never-ending plains.

In the slab-built, zinc-roofed homestead of some lately-taken run,
In the tent beside the bankment of a railway just begun,
In the huts on new selection, in the camps of man's unrest,
On the frontiers of the Nation, live the Women of the West.

The red sun robs their beauty, and, in weariness and pain,
The slow years steal the nameless grace that never comes again;
And there are hours men cannot soothe, and words men cannot say—
The nearest woman's face may be a hundred miles away.

The wide bush holds the secrets of their longings and desires,
When the white stars in reverence light holy altar-fires,
And silence, like the touch of God, sinks deep into the breast—
Perchance He hears and understands the Women of the West.

For them no trumpet sounds the call, no poet plies his arts—
They only hear the beating of their gallant loving hearts.
But they have sung with silent lives the song all songs above—
The holiness of sacrifice, the dignity of love.

Well have we held our father's creed. No call has passed us by.
We faced and fought the wilderness, we sent our sons to die.
And we have hearts to do and dare, and yet, o'er all the rest,
The hearts that made the Nation were the Women of the West.

GEORGE ESSEX EVANS

WHEN DACEY RODE THE MULE

'Twas in a small, up-country town,
    When we were boys at school,
There came a circus with a clown
    And with a bucking mule.
The clown announced a scheme they had—
    The mule was such a king
They'd give a crown to any lad
    Who'd ride him round the ring.
And, gentle reader, do not scoff
    Nor think the man a fool,
To buck a porous plaster off
    Was pastime to that mule.

The boys got on—he bucked like sin—
    He threw them in the dirt.
And then the clown would raise a grin
    But Johnny Dacey came one night,
    The crack of all the school,
Said he, 'I'll win the crown all right,
    Bring in your bucking mule.'
The elephant went off his trunk,
    The monkey played the fool,
And all the band got blazing drunk
    When Dacey rode the mule.

But soon there rose an awful shout
    Of laughter, when the clown,
From somewhere in his pants drew out
    A little paper crown.
He placed the crown on Dacey's head,
    While Dacey looked a fool,
'Now, there's your crown, my lad,' he said,
    'For riding of the mule!'
The band struck up with 'Killaloe',
    And 'Rule Britannia, Rule',
And 'Young Man from the Country', too,
    When Dacey rode the mule.

Then Dacey, in a furious rage,
    For vengeance on the show
Ascended to the monkeys' cage
    And let the monkeys go;
The blue-tailed ape and chimpanzee
    He turned abroad to roam;
Good faith! It was a sight to see
    The people step for home.
For big baboons with canine snout
    Are spiteful, as a rule,
The people didn't sit it out
    When Dacey rode the mule.

And from the beasts that did escape
    The bushmen all declare
Were born some creatures partly ape
    And partly native bear.
They're rather few and far between;
    The race is nearly spent;
But some of them may still be seen
    In Sydney Parliament.
And when those legislators fight,
    And drink, and act the fool—
It all commenced that wretched night
    When Dacey rode the mule.

A.B. PATERSON

Out Back

The old year went, and the new returned, in the
    withering weeks of drought,
The cheque was spent that the shearer earned, and the
    sheds were all cut out;
The publican's words were short and few, and the
    publican's looks were black—
And the time had come as the shearer knew, to carry
    his swag Out Back.

For time means tucker, and tramp you must, where the scrubs and
    plains are wide,
With seldom a track that a man can trust, or a mountain peak
    to guide;
All day long in the dust and heat—when summer is on the
    track—
With stinted stomachs and blistered feet, they carry their swags
    Out Back.

He tramped away from the shanty there, where the days
    were long and hot,
With never a soul to know or care if he died on the
    track or not.
The poor of the city have friends in woe, no matter
    how much they lack,
But only God and the swagmen know how a poor man
    fares Out Back.

He begged his way on the parched Paroo and the
    Warrego tracks once more,
And lived like a dog, as the swagmen do, till the
    Western stations shore;
But men were many, and sheds were full, for work in
    the town was slack—
The traveller never got hands in wool, though he
    tramped for a year Out Back.

In stifling noons when his back was wrung by its load,
    and the air seemed dead,
And the water warmed in the bag that hung to his
    aching arm like lead,
Or in times of flood, when plains were seas, and the
    scrubs were cold and black,
He ploughed in mud to his trembling knees, and paid for
    his sins Out Back.

He blamed himself in the year 'Too Late'—in the heaviest
    hours of life—
'Twas little he dreamed that a shearing-mate had care of his
    home and wife;
There are times when wrongs from your kindred come, and
    treacherous tongues attack—
When a man is better away from home, and dead to the
    world, Out Back.

And dirty and careless and old he wore, as his lamp of hope
    grew dim;
He tramped for years till the swag he bore seemed part of
    himself to him.
As bullock drags in the sandy ruts, he followed the dreary
    track,
With never a thought but to reach the huts when the sun
    went down Out Back.

It chanced one day, when the north wind blew in his face
    like a furnace-breath,
He left the track for a tank he knew—'twas a short-cut to his
    death;
For the bed of the tank was hard and dry, and crossed with
    many a crack,
And, oh! it's a terrible thing to die of thirst in the scrub
    Out Back.

A drover came, but the fringe of law was eastward many
    a mile;
He never reported the thing he saw, for it was not worth
    his while.
The tanks are full and the grass is high in the mulga off
    the track,
Where the bleaching bones of a white man lie by his
    mouldering swag Out Back.

For time means tucker, and tramp they must, where the plains
    and scrubs are wide,
With seldom a track that a man can trust, or a mountain peak
    to guide;
All day long in the flies and heat the men of the outside track
With stinted stomachs and blistered feet must carry their swags
    Out Back.

Henry Lawson

THE FITZROY BLACKSMITH

With Apologies to Longfellow

Under the spreading deficit,
    The Fitzroy Smithy stands;
The smith, a spendthrift man is he,
    With too much on his hands;
But the muscles of his brawny jaw
    Are strong as iron bands.

Pay out, pay out, from morn till night,
    You can hear the sovereigns go;
Or you'll hear him singing 'Old Folks at Home',
    In a deep bass voice and slow,
Like a bullfrog down in the village well
    When the evening sun is low.

The Australian going 'home' for loans
    Looks in at the open door;
He loves to see the imported plant,
    And to hear the furnace roar,
And to watch the private firms smash up
    Like chaff on the threshing-floor.

Toiling, rejoicing, borrowing,
    Onward through life he goes;
Each morning sees some scheme begun
    That never sees its close.
Something unpaid for, someone done,
    Has earned a night's repose.

The Fitzroy Blacksmith
Alfred Deakin (1856–1919),
second Prime Minister of Australia.

A.B. PATERSON

HOW MCDOUGAL TOPPED THE SCORE

A peaceful spot is Piper's Flat. The folk that live around—
They keep themselves by keeping sheep and turning up the ground;
But the climate is erratic, and the consequences are
The struggle with the elements is everlasting war.
We plough, and sow, and harrow—then sit down and pray for rain;
And then we all get flooded out and have to start again.
But the folk are now rejoicing as they ne'er rejoiced before,
For we've played Molongo cricket, and McDougal topped the score!

Molongo had a head on it, and challenged us to play
A single-innings match for lunch—the losing team to pay.
We were not great guns at cricket, but we couldn't well say no,
So we all began to practise, and we let the reaping go.
We scoured the Flat for ten miles round to muster up our men,
But when the list was totalled we could only number ten.
Then up spoke big Tim Brady: he was always slow to speak,
And he said—'What price McDougal, who lives down at
    Cooper's Creek?'

So we sent for old McDougal, and he stated in reply
That he'd never played at cricket, but he'd half a mind to try.
He couldn't come to practise—he was getting in his hay,
But he guessed he'd show the beggars from Molongo how to play.
Now, McDougal was a Scotchman, and a canny one at that,
So he started in to practise with a paling for a bat.
He got Mrs Mac to bowl to him, but she couldn't run at all,
So he trained his sheep-dog, Pincher, how to scout and fetch the ball.

Now, Pincher was no puppy; he was old, and worn, and grey;
But he understood McDougal, and— accustomed to obey—
When McDougal cried out 'Fetch it!' he would fetch it in a trice,
But, until the word was 'Drop it!' he would grip it like a vice.
And each succeeding night they played until the light grew dim:
Sometimes McDougal struck the ball—sometimes the ball
    struck him.
Each time he struck, the ball would plough a furrow in the ground;
And when he missed, the impetus would turn him three times round.

The fatal day at length arrived—the day that was to see
Molongo bite the dust, or Piper's Flat knocked up a tree!
Molongo's captain won the toss, and sent his men to bat,
And they gave some leather-hunting to the men of Piper's Flat.

When the ball sped where McDougal stood, firm planted in his track,
He shut his eyes, and turned him round, and stopped it—
    with his back!
The highest score was twenty-two, the total sixty-six,
When Brady sent a yorker down that scattered Johnson's sticks.

Then Piper's Flat went in to bat, for glory and renown,
But, like the grass before the scythe, our wickets tumbled down.
'Nine wickets down for seventeen, with fifty more to win!'
Our captain heaved a heavy sigh, and sent McDougal in.
'Ten pounds to one you'll lose it!' cried a barracker from town;
But McDougal said, 'I'll tak' it, mon!' and planked the money down.
Then he girded up his moleskins in a self-reliant style,
Threw off his hat and boots and faced the bowler with a smile.

He held the bat the wrong side out, and Johnson with a grin
Stepped lightly to the bowling crease, and sent a 'wobbler' in;
McDougal spooned it softly back, and Johnson waited there,
But McDougal, crying 'Fetch it!' started running like a hare.
Molongo shouted 'Victory! He's out as sure as eggs,'
When Pincher started through the crowd, and ran through
    Johnson's legs.
He seized the ball like lightning; then he ran behind a log,
And McDougal kept on running, while Molongo chased the dog!

They chased him up, they chased him down, they chased him
    round, and then
He darted through the sliprail as the scorer shouted 'Ten!'
McDougal puffed; Molongo swore; excitement was intense;
As the scorer marked down twenty, Pincher cleared a barbed-wire fence.

'Let us head him!' shrieked Molongo. 'Brain the mongrel with a bat!'
'Run it out! Good old McDougal!' yelled the men of Piper's Flat.
And McDougal kept on jogging, and then Pincher doubled back,
And the scorer counted 'Forty' as they raced across the track.

McDougal's legs were going fast, Molongo's breath was gone—
But still Molongo chased the dog— McDougal struggled on.
When the scorer shouted 'Fifty' then they knew the chase
   could cease;
And McDougal gasped out 'Drop it!' as he dropped within his crease.
Then Pincher dropped the ball, and as instinctively he knew
Discretion was the wiser plan, he disappeared from view;
And as Molongo's beaten men exhausted lay around
We raised McDougal shoulder-high, and bore him from the ground.

We bore him to McGinniss's, where lunch was ready laid,
And filled him up with whisky-punch, for which Molongo paid.
We drank his health in bumpers and we cheered him three times three,
And when Molongo got its breath Molongo joined the spree.

And the critics say they never saw a cricket match like that,
When McDougal broke the record in the game at Piper's Flat,
And the folk are jubilating as they never did before;
For we played Molongo cricket— and McDougal topped the score!

THOMAS E. SPENCER

63

First published by
New Holland Publishers (Australia)

National Library Cataloguing-in-Publication data

Favourite Australian Poems

ISBN 1 86436 059 3

1. Australian poetry. 2. Australia–Poetry
I. Newell, Rex

A821.00803294

New Holland Publishers (Australia)
A division of National Book Distributors Pty Ltd
3/2 Aquatic Drive, Frenchs Forest, NSW 2086, Australia

Introduction by Chris Mansell
Designed and typeset by ANACONDA GRAPHIC DESIGN
Publishing Department Manager: Jane Hazell
Publisher: Sally Bird
Reproduction by: Litho Platemakers Pty Ltd
Printed and bound by: Griffin Press, South Australia